I Love
Tractors, trucks, diggers, and dumpers

Castle Street PRESS

Big rig

Big rigs are great at hauling material from one place to another. A big rig is made up of a **tractor unit** and a **trailer**.

sleeping compartment

headlight

fender

Trailers

A big rig's **trailer** holds a **heavy load**. Trailers can carry many things, from logs to fuel.

trailer

mirror

.......fuel tank

Mad about big rigs

The biggest trucks weigh 80,000 lb (36,300 kg)—that's as much as 80 polar bears!

Some rigs are so big they have their own bedroom!

This rig is as strong as 600 horses!

Some people are so mad about their trucks they enter them into big rig beauty contests!

Dump truck

Dump trucks can carry heavy loads of soil, sand, and rubble in their **dump truck body**. They are so powerful that they can drive easily over muddy construction sites and roads.

dump
truck body

Big lifter

The **dump truck**'s strong **body** can lift up in just 12 seconds in order to tip out its load.

tipping out the load

off-road tire

cab

grille

fender

chassis

Mad about dumpers

This dump truck can carry the weight of over 1,000 children or 200,000 hamburgers!

Cement truck

cement

The **cement truck** prepares cement to be taken to construction sites. The giant **mixer** spins around to keep the cement from drying out.

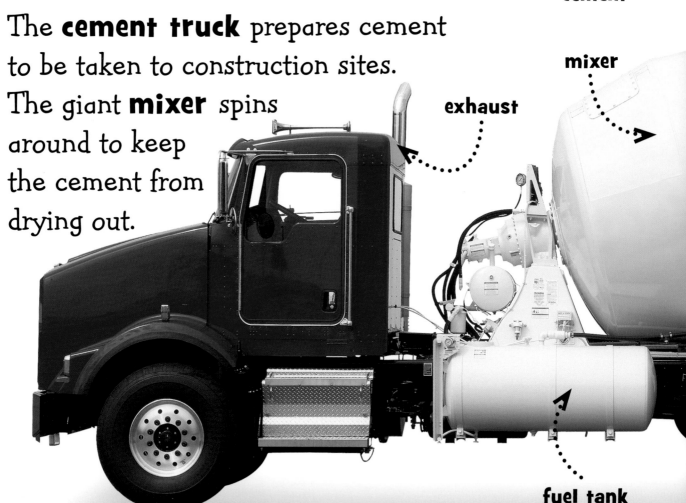

exhaust

mixer

fuel tank

hopper

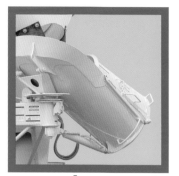

chute

Unloading

The **chute** can move in different directions to drop the **cement** where it's needed.

...... hopper

...... chute

Mad about cement trucks

An average cement mixer could hold the contents of over 17,000 cans of soda.

A man from China became famous when he built his house out of two massive cement pipes!

Snowplow

Snowplows work hard to clear heavy **snowdrifts** from the roads. The plow attaches to the front of different trucks.

V-shaped plow

Clear it up!
V-shaped plows can push **snow** to each side to move it out of the way.

Mad about snowplows

Snowdrifts are big mounds of snow piled up by the wind. In the Antarctic, snowdrifts can be taller than houses!

The biggest snowman in the world was built in 2008. It was over 120 ft (36 m) tall.

exhaust

snowdrift

plow blade

Backhoe loader

Backhoe loaders have a big **shovel** attached to the front and a strong **bucket** in the back. The shovel can scoop up heavy loads, while the bucket can dig deep into the ground.

work lights

cab

shovel

boom

tire

Two jobs at once!

The driver's **seat** swivels from back to front, so that he can use either the **bucket** or the **shovel**.

controls

bucket

Mad about backhoes

The bucket can dig down to a depth of 14 ft (4.3 m).

The bright work lights mean that the driver can work all through the night.

The shovel can lift 3.47 tons (3,154 kg), which is as heavy as an adult hippo or two small cars!

Tractor

Tractors are ready to tackle all types of tough jobs! They have **thick tires** to carry them across muddy, bumpy ground and a **powerful engine** to help them lift and move heavy loads.

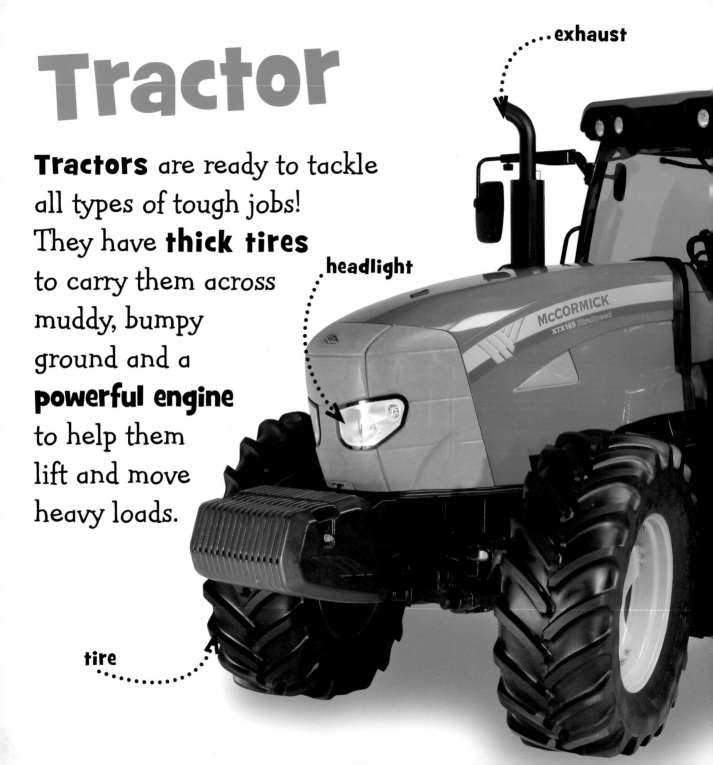

exhaust

headlight

tire

flashing light

Plow it up

Tractors pull **plows** across the fields to make the soil ready for new seeds.

plow

steering wheel

Mad about tractors

Some people are so crazy about tractors that they have special tractor races.

This tractor is about as tall as three children!

rear wheel

Giant tractor

This **giant tracked tractor** is a massive machine. It can haul heavy **plows** and **big drills** across the farmer's fields.

cab

wheel

rubber tracks

steps

rubber track

Rubber tracks

The big **rubber tracks** spread out the tractor's enormous **weight**.

Mad about tractors

This tractor can lift the weight of two small elephants!

It weighs nearly 20 tons (18,000 kg), which is the same as two school buses.

It has the pulling power of 543 horses.

This tractor is so big it needs steps on the side so the driver can get in!

Combine harvester

Combine harvesters are hard workers! Farmers use them to complete their **crop harvests**. They have special **computers**, which make sure they work very accurately.

unloading grain

controls

Mad about combines

Modern combines can harvest up to 60 tons (54,000 kg) of grain an hour. That's enough to make half a million sandwiches!

Some people are so mad about their crops that they build massive corn mazes. The world's biggest corn maze was built in 2007 and is larger than 33 football fields.

computer system

unloading
tube

cab

revolving reel

Search the scene. Try to find . . .

2 tractors

3 dump trucks

I cement truck

2 backhoe loaders

6 tires

Big digger spotting!

Guess who?

Look at the pictures, read the clues, and guess what each truck or tractor is.

1  My mixer drum turns and turns as I drive to the building site.

2  My big, thick tires make it easy to drive over rough, bumpy ground.

3  My tractor unit does the pulling while my trailer carries the load.

4  With a shovel at the front and a bucket at the back, I work very hard.

5  I tip up in order to empty heavy loads out onto the ground.

6 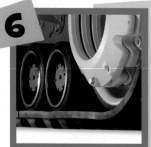 Rubber tracks help to spread out my very heavy weight.

Answers: 1. Cement truck; 2. Tractor; 3. Big rig; 4. Backhoe loader; 5. Dump truck; 6. Giant tractor.